# Home

# Home

## *Portraits from the Carolina Coast*

*To Barbara
A dear friend,
2007*

## Vennie Deas Moore

### with

## William Baldwin

Additional editing by V. Elizabeth Turk

Charleston    London

History
PRESS

Published by The History Press
18 Percy Street
Charleston, SC 29403
866.223.5778
www.historypress.net

All cover images by Vennie Deas Moore.

Additional editing by V. Elizabeth Turk.

First published 2006

Manufactured in the United Kingdom

ISBN 1.59629.093.5

Library of Congress Cataloging-in-Publication Data

Moore, Vennie Deas.
Home : portraits from the Carolina coast / Vennie Deas Moore with William
Baldwin.
p. cm.
ISBN 1-59629-093-5 (alk. paper)
1. Coasts--South Carolina--Pictorial works. 2. South Carolina--Pictorial
works. 3. South Carolina--Economic conditions--Pictorial works. 4. South
Carolina--Social life and customs--Pictorial works. 5. African
Americans--South Carolina--Pictorial works. I. Baldwin, William P. II.
Title.
F270.M66 2006
975.70022'2--dc22
2005036394

To my brother, Henry "Bub" Deas Jr.

I was raised away from home. I was off living in Charleston with my aunt. But I wasn't completely cut off from my family. I went home for visits. My mama came to see me. My father and brothers would ride the graveyard-shift bus in to work at the navy yard. They would come to see me. Then my brother Bub went to high school in Charleston. He rode the bus. I'd see him at school. He was looking after me. I was college bound; he was in the trade school at Burke, so we didn't share classes. And he was shy, too shy to say much, but he looked after me. I'd see him watching in the schoolyard from a distance.

He went to Vietnam as a Green Beret. And he made it possible for me to go to college by sending me his military allotment. He wasn't married then. He's married now. Four children of his own. He was and is a good man. And he went off to war. He still has shrapnel in his body. He won a purple heart. I dedicate this book to my brother Bub.

# Contents

# Foreword

"Vennie Deas Moore has the eye of a poet and the heart of a lioness…a timid lioness, but a lioness nonetheless." I wrote that about Vennie several years ago, and it's still true. She tells me that next spring she's headed off alone to China and then Japan. Lord knows it takes courage to put yourself in strange surroundings—to go to Africa as she's already done, to leave home and see what's out there. But Vennie has another kind of courage, as well. She's willing to face the familiar, which often requires even more of the journeyer, and, for the most part, that is what the following photography collection is concerned with—that poetry of the familiar, which she's still explaining to me.

Still. Five days ago when I suggested discarding a particular photograph for a reason other than aesthetic she replied, "Oh, there're just people." Then she smiled and added three additional words of explanation: "People, people, people."

I first met Vennie in the mid-'80s, but only knew her to say hello. We were both born in McClellanville, South Carolina, and both of us were then brought up in other communities. For both of us McClellanville has remained a touchstone. I live there now. She lives midstate, in Columbia. In 1997 we'd gotten together for lunch (at the diner pictured in this book). She explained how she'd spent her adult life raising a family, getting her two sons grown and educated, and to do this she had worked as a medical technologist for the Red Cross. With the graduation of the youngest she had quit her job. She wanted to do something else. Something, but she wasn't sure what. Walking out of the restaurant she said, "I want to do something that matters."

Of course, caring for her sons did matter. Quite obviously it was the most important thing in her life, but I did understand what she meant. She wanted to make an impression, to contribute to that great and usually indifferent world of the arts and sciences. So, there on the sidewalk, I suggested that she take some more photographs. She'd just finished up the Sandy Island series, and I'd seen several of those. She said she would like to and I suggested that she work under the direction of McClellanville's newly formed Village Museum. We went and struck a deal with museum director Selden Hill and museum board member Patty Fulcher. Vennie would photograph the local seafood industry and other "local" subjects and the museum (always operating on less than adequate funding) would develop and print the photographs and pay Vennie's bus fare here and back to Columbia. Vennie didn't drive, at least not distances.

So, not long after, Vennie Deas Moore rode the bus down from Columbia (eight hours to cover 150 miles), went oystering (ten hours to cover 30 miles) and then rode straight back to Columbia on the bus (another eight hours). I was impressed—by both her endurance and the photographs. She continued in this manner for another three years, and the majority of the photographs shown here are taken from the resulting Village Museum collections.

But the above is only the "how and why" of a documentary project and has a limited relationship to Vennie as an artist. From the beginning, I was struck with her uncanny ability to frame the space within a viewfinder, to quite literally recognize what mattered visually. You can see this quickly enough in the Pawleys Island prints, especially those containing the pier and groins where there's a quirky juxtaposition of people and angular construction that I don't think can be taught. It's simply come upon…or perhaps desired in some truly intense way. Intensely desired. I've seen the word "talent" defined in those words.

In addition, Vennie has a strong narrative sense. Often she tells a story with a single shot—a child dancing in the surf or a man at work or a ball player about to steal second—but nowhere is this clearer than in the grouped shots included here. We've left those in proof sheet form (bracketed by the film edge) to suggest the action involved—the importance of what happened next.

And of course, I should mention Vennie's ability to relate to people with her camera; that is her uncanny gift for portraits. You can see it clearly in the earliest of these photographs, those taken in Africa. "They were so interested in me and the camera," Vennie says. "They would come up and look right at me." A dozen years have passed and she's long since back on the North American continent, but it seems that people still respond that way.

I've thought about this. I've watched Vennie taking portraits, watched the intensity on the subject's face (whether smile or frown) and the photographer's equally earnest concern with the camera—*cameras* I should say. In Africa she was using a traditional 35-mm and that recent photograph of her mother by the hydrangea was done with a small digital camera, but the majority of these portraits (and the seafood documentation) was done with an old "junk store" Rolleiflex, the twin-lens, 2¼-negative sort abandoned back in the 1950s. And I've come to the conclusion that it's Vennie peering down into the viewfinder that draws the subject's attention in such a distinct and usually trusting manner—that and, of course, the fact that this small, African American woman is indeed interested in them…in them as people. Or as Vennie puts it: "People, people, people."

We at McClellanville's Village Museum are proud to have played a part in Vennie's "something that matters" project. We hope you enjoy what follows.

William Baldwin
2005

# Acknowledgements

*Thanks to the following: The Village Museum, The Gaylord and Dorothy Donnelley Foundation, The McKissick Museum, Hampton Plantation State Park and The Endocrine Foundation. And thanks to Selden "Bud" Hill, Patty Fulcher, Gary Bronson and Elizabeth Turk for their assistance, and to Kirsty Sutton, Jason Chasteen and the entire staff of The History Press for another job well done. And, of course, a special thanks to all those pictured here.*

*W.B.*

Thanks to photographers Hunter Clarkson, Gordon Brown and Susan Dugan. For professional assistance, thanks to William Baldwin, Lynn Robertson and Carl Steen; for organizational assistance, the Village Museum and McKissick Museum; and for encouragement, Genevieve Peterkin, Eugenia P. Deas and Mayor Rutledge Leland.

Thanks also to the wonderful coastal communities of Sandy Island, Germantown, Santee, McClellanville, Awendaw and Georgetown, South Carolina.

# Introduction: The Carolina Coast

My name is Vennie Deas Moore. As a photographer I am largely self-taught. I am an African American woman—though I think of myself as simply "me." I am in my midfifties. I was born and raised in what is called the South Carolina Lowcountry.

Along the coast both north and south of Charleston there are many small communities of slave descendants. Until the 1930s these hamlets were connected to the rest of the world only by narrow dirt roads. This isolation meant that outside influences were kept to a minimum. Even today, many dietary, medical and cultural practices of these neighborhoods can be linked to those of their West African ancestors. The most obvious example is Gullah, a Creole language still spoken among the oldest of the people—and some of the youngest. Part African and part seventeenth-century English, this was the language spoken as our ancestors toiled in the rice and cotton fields. It's a protective language, one that, even today, only the members of a community can understand. There is a second language, English, for the outside world.

But Gullah is not a language linked to despair. It is linked to joy, a joy that can be heard especially in the gospel music of the churches or on the front porch of a small shotgun cabin like my mama's. And it's the language that some school children can still speak. When I was teaching at Choppee, just above Georgetown, I heard them speak this among themselves while in the breezeway. Once in the classroom they code switched into Standard English. What you say about the Gullah language can also be said about the Gullah culture. It can protect a whole community—protect and define who a people are. But once that capsule is broken you're wide open to the world around.

My home (my first home) is forty miles north of Charleston in McClellanville. I live in the state capital of Columbia now, but my mama still lives on Society Road just north of McClellanville. This is the black neighborhood. The village of McClellanville is the white neighborhood. I went four years to the all-black Johnson C. Smith University and received a pre-med degree, but after that my entire adult life was spent in an integrated environment. I went next to the South Carolina Medical University, which was almost all white, and then George Washington University that was the same. Then I worked with the Red Cross for more than ten years as a disaster volunteer.

Of course, I can't call any of this a really integrated environment. I was usually the only black. That's a strange feeling. But I can forget I'm black unless I stick my hand out and look at it. I'm seeing white. Like anthropologist Zora Neale Hurston says, "at certain times I have no race, I am me." Then I come home. Black is black again and white is white. I don't think black and white will ever be free of each other. Last year a friend of my brother's walked me down Society Road. I got to the first oak tree on the village main street, Pinckney Street, and I realized I was talking to myself. He had stopped at the first oak. That was the line of demarcation. An invisible wall. I had to go back to finish the conversation. That was a couple of years ago. I took my mama to a presentation in Georgetown. They had mint julep tea and she wouldn't drink it because that's what she served when she worked in white houses. The connotation, the connections she made between tea and service—another line of demarcation.

Black or white, the communities are still isolated. They are isolated from each other and they are still isolated from the outside world. Despite the paved roads they stay cut off, to a degree. People may commute long-distance on the paved roads but when they get home at night they are still in a different world. And if they stay and work in their community they are still in a different world because they are doing jobs that are quickly vanishing. I tried to document that. Shrimping, picking oysters, crabbing, working in a crab factory or heading and packing shrimp, fishing for shad or working in a lumber mill. When not working the people have their good times; the church services, reunions, parades, ball games and other events that bring the community together. I've tried to cover that, and not just in McClellanville, but in Sandy Island, Santee and other small places along the coast.

I have also included photographs I took in Africa twelve years ago. These reminded me of home in a way. I was often told that as long as I didn't open my mouth to speak, I was taken for an African woman. I take that as a compliment. Of course, these photographs are directly related to our Gullah culture.

The South Carolina Lowcountry as I knew it as a child is threatened. Heirs' property, land shared by all, is the tradition of the Gullah culture. The oldest keeps the land and then gives portions to the children when they come of age. There is no line of demarcation, no fences. The elder of the extended family is the ruler over this, just as it would be in Africa. As far as the old Gullah community is concerned this was fine. But you have two worlds bumping up against each other. And in the other world, this sharing of land without deeds is not legal. Court cases can resolve the situation and when this happens it's usually a wealthy developer who receives the land. Just having to pay the rising property taxes can do the same thing. More and more, the people of the land are being displaced.

Also the sense of self-sufficiency is being eroded. Before, those in the black communities had land to grow their crops, they harvested seafood, went hunting. They kept cattle and sheep. You didn't go hungry. You had a unity—one for all and all for one. If you had, everyone had. There was a sense of total sharing. And children were shared by everyone in the family. Everyone in the community was responsible for the children. Cousins, grandmothers, sisters and brothers, they were all sharing the family's responsibilities. My mama is one of those sisters; one of those Da's, a lead mother in the community. They call her Sister Eugenia, but there's less and less of that today.

So many of the people are leaving the Gullah communities. People like me. When I left it, I left it. Those in my generation went off to college, schools or military service, and some did come back home. And this wasn't just a question of money. They wanted to be home. They were making the kind of money that they could have lived anywhere. But others like me let go of home. We went. But I won't say we went for a better life or that we wanted more. I don't think more is necessarily more. I won't say I'm envious of those who stayed, but I do regret my loss of connectedness, and that's the purpose of this work. I wanted so badly to connect.

This book features photographs and journal entries from over a dozen years. It will take the viewer on a journey back in time. Photographer Elizabeth Turk, who helped to edit this book, says that's the job of photography, "to mirror life and suspend time." It's a special power, this freezing of the moment with just the click of a lens. That's the impossible job a photographer tries to do.

What follows is my attempt to capture a vanishing Lowcountry culture. To leave a record. To show a people at home.

But I realized at the same time that I am dealing with myself, with my own mortality.

Through their eyes,
I see
Generations pass.

Through their faces,
I see
Toils and peace.

# Book One

# People of the Creek

# Shrimping

Shrimp season in this area runs roughly from mid-May to the end of December, with the most productive months being the white shrimp run of September and October. Boats often leave the dock for a week at a time, but just as commonly they go and come every day, which is the sort of trip Vennie made here. Before entering the ocean, the outriggers are lowered on each side and, once "outside," the doors and nets are drug into the water, and then the forward momentum of the boat causes the doors to sink and spread the net wide. The captain runs the winch and the striker does the rest.

A tow lasts about two hours, but small samplings are made with the try net every fifteen minutes or so. Once the nets are hauled back the bags are swung on board and emptied. Then the striker (the deck hand) is responsible for culling out the shrimp from the trash, washing the shrimp and icing them below deck. This he does while the captain tries to figure out where the shrimp will show up next. After four tows it's back inside where the doors and nets are pulled on board, the outriggers are raised and the boat makes the five-mile return trip to the dock.

At the dock the shrimp are loaded into baskets and brought into a large room where they're headed, washed and sorted, and then sent on to seafood restaurants and the like.

In the years since these photographs were taken the shrimping industry has had to endure a variety of economic assaults, but many captains are still going out—including the one pictured here. Thanks to him and his striker for their good-natured patience.

Below is Vennie's impression of the trip.

W.B.

It's 4:00 a.m. in early June. I go down to the dock. For some time I have been asking Mayor Rutledge Leland to let me go out on one of the shrimp boats. He is not only the lifetime mayor of the Village, but a boat and seafood company owner. On this calm morning my mother and Mayor Leland stand on the edge of the pier. The men help me to climb onto the trawler. I lose my footing on the deck. Mayor Leland yells at me, "I better not hear you took off that life jacket!" My mother yells at the captain, "You better bring her home safe!" I wave goodbye as the trawler heads for open water.

We slowly travel the creek. Small waves break on the shore. The dark nets hang heavy in the salt air. The striker begins to lower them. The stillness of dawn is filled with the sound of the engine. In the wheelhouse the captain communicates to other captains on the shortwave radio. They compare where the big catches were made the day before. How far must he go today? The quiet of the creek is further broken by rock-and-roll music coming over the radio. Finished, the striker lies on his back and watches the sea gulls. They follow the trawler. In time they too will feed off the day's catch.

Now porpoises play hide-and-seek off the bow. We enter the ocean. The nets enter the water. We begin to tow. A trail of muddy water marks our path. The sun has fully risen and I begin to photograph.

Shrimp boats. *McClellanville, 1999*

Dawn on the ocean. *Cape Romain, 1998*

Striker casting to retrieve the small try net. *Cape Romain, 1998*

Captain heads the try-net shrimp.
*Cape Romain, 1998*

Breakfast from the try net.
*Cape Romain, 1998*

Sea gulls.
*Cape Romain, 1998*

Everybody waits for the catch—gulls too.
*Cape Romain, 1998*

Hauling back. The turtle extractor above the bag lets the loggerheads escape. *Cape Romain, 1998*

First catch on the deck. The cull pile is pushed together. *Cape Romain, 1998*

Sorting the shrimp from the rest. *Cape Romain, 1998*

Outriggers with perching gulls. Washing down the deck. *Cape Romain, 1998*

Captain in the wheelhouse. *Cape Romain, 1998*

More tows to cull.
*Cape Romain, 1998*

Time for a rest.
*Cape Romain, 1998*

End of the day. *Cape Romain, 1998*

Bringing the doors on deck. *Cape Romain, 1998*

"My mama said it would kill her to see me in the ocean. So I chose to work the dock." *McClellanville, 1999*

Trawlers reflecting. *McClellanville, 1999*

Preparing the catch for shipping.
*McClellanville, 1999*

Dumping on the heading table.
*McClellanville, 1999*

Heading shrimp. *McClellanville, 1999*

Talking about webbing.
*McClellanville, 1999*

Adjusting the chain.
*McClellanville, 1999*

What's going on down there?
*McClellanville, 2000*

On the sea for many years.
*McClellanville, 2001*

Hardened by the sea. *McClellanville, 1998*

Pelicans resting. *McClellanville, 1998*

# Oystering

*Oysters are picked in the cool of the year—as the saying goes: those months whose names have an r in them. Since the local oyster grounds have been heavily harvested, the oyster crew often tows three hours down the inland waterway to better grounds about fifteen miles to the south.*

*Once there, the twenty-foot bateaux disperse, usually one man to each, and for the last two hours of the receding tide and the first hour of the flood the pickers work, quickly tossing the oysters from bank to boat. The oysters are culled as they go, the dead shell being knocked aside, but often further culling is done on the return trip. It's usually late at night before the last boat has been shoveled out at the dock, and the next trip out can start even before daylight. It's hard, hard work, especially on those freezing northeaster days when the tide's not going to drop but groceries are still to be bought.*

*Like the shrimping, the oystering industry has had to struggle along over the last several years. Some time back oysters were shucked in McClellanville, but now it's oyster roasts and the like that serve the catch.*

*W.B.*

The towboat pulled the empty bateau out to the oystering grounds. Early morning—early. Boats trailing behind. The men eat breakfast, sleep. Once anchored they go quickly—all in sync. They yank the tie-up ropes, crank their outboard motors and they're gone out across the bay.

I tell the captain I'm supposed to go out. He says, "Oh." Turns out one was left, my cousin and his fiberglass boat. I asked why I couldn't go on a traditional wooden boat, a bateau, and he says, "Well, the fiberglass boat won't sink." I'm disappointed, but they are looking out for me. A fiberglass boat has floatation.

My cousin worked without stopping. Pulled the boat along the shore. Didn't take a lunch break. Didn't stop to wipe the sweat or remove the mud. He stopped for nothing. He had to fill the whole boat up with oysters while the tide was out. Forty bushels or more. He flung them in. (I too threw in a couple of oysters.) Most of this was stoop work, bending at the waist.

The mud is often soft. Pluff mud with marsh grass sticking out. He got through before the tide came in. The boat was on the bank so we waited for it to float. The men ate when they got back. They heated their lunch buckets on the towboat stove. Some ate oysters.

Going home with the winter sun low. Oyster beds are covered; loaded bateaux are deep in the water. I go home at dark—I'd survived. I was so excited that I had made it through. When I'd asked how deep the water was, somebody said, "If it's over six feet it doesn't matter." I was frightened the whole time. I never learned to swim. I didn't wear a life jacket and should have.

I was thankful that we hadn't had bad weather. This was a nice day.

The tow boat. *McClellanville, 1998*

Leaving Jeremy Creek. Early morning and empty bateaux get towed to the oyster grounds. *McClellanville, 1998*

Washing the pot after breakfast. *Sewee Bay, 1998*

No time to stop. *Sewee Bay, 1998*

Tossing oysters into the bateau. *Sewee Bay, 1998*

Leaning down to pick oysters. *Sewee Bay, 1998*

First set of bateaux get ready to haul home. *Sewee Bay, 1998*

The last boat to attach. *Sewee Bay, 1998*

Late night shoveling out the oysters. The end of a twelve-hour day. *McClellanville, 1998*

Oysterman. *McClellanville, 1999*

# Crabbing

*Except in the hardest of winters, the crabbers can be found running their pots—anywhere from 50 to 150 in the local Cape Romain marshes. Each of these wire traps has a bait basket in the center to which the crab finds its way through a funnel opening. Once in, he or she feeds and then swims upward into a second chamber and can't get out.*

*Usually the crabber pulls his pots every day, dumps the catch into a sorting box, removes the conchs, flounder and "too small" crabs, and sets the rest aside in boxes or baskets. The crabbers here were working basket crabs (those sent north to the restaurants), as well as peeler crabs—the crabs about to shed their hard shells and thus become the desirable "soft shells" that end up in deep fryers.*

*The crab-picking plant shown here often depended on trawl crabs and other crabs from off. As with shrimping and oystering, the crabbing industry has taken some hard knocks in recent years. This plant has since closed down and the site was turned into waterfront residential lots.*

*W.B.*

As a child I crabbed with my uncle under Charleston's Cooper River bridge. Threw out a chicken neck on a line, pulled it in slowly and scooped the crab up with a net on a stick. I was always afraid the crab would catch one of my toes. We'd take them home and cook them. That was crabbing. Commercial crabbing was something else.

What interested me most was the calmness of the water and the bobbing of the milk-jug floats that mark the sunken traps. Then the crabber arrives. He keeps the boat going in a circle as he pulls the pot.

One thing about crabbing always tickles me. Mama says the members of the black community are like the crabs. They latch on to each other. They hold on to each other so nobody can go out. She says we act like crabs. In a bad way. We pull each other down.

The women at the crab company were a hard group to photograph. Sanitation was a problem—it was a sterile environment. I had to get wrapped in white and wear a net. And the women think of their workplace as private. They weren't ashamed of working but they didn't want to be seen in work clothes. They are churchwomen and prefer to be seen in church clothes.

The saddest part was to go back two years later and the crab ladies weren't there. And then to go back two years after that and the crab company buildings weren't there. It's all changed. Even the oyster towboat has been sold.

Crabbing creeks. Horsehead tower. *Cape Romain, 1998*

Clinging crabs. *Cape Romain, 1998*

Trapping—pulling the pot and throwing it back. *Cape Romain, 1998*

Crabber. *Cape Romain, 1998*

Looking for peeler crabs. *Cape Romain, 1998*

Finding a peeler. *Cape Romain, 1998*

This dock does peeler crabs and basket crabs. *McClellanville, 1999*

Crabber. *McClellanville, 1999*

On the "house boat." *McClellanville, 1999*

This dock cooks the crabs and picks the meat.
*McClellanville, 1999*

Steaming the crabs.
*McClellanville, 1999*

White walls, women in white. *McClellanville, 1999*

Picking crabs. *McClellanville, 1999*

Packing crab meat. *McClellanville, 1999*

Claw meat. *McClellanville, 1999*

Crab dock on a stormy day. *McClellanville, 1999*

Rolleiflex camera—self-portrait. *McClellanville, 1999*

# Book Two

# People of the Land

# Sandy Island

Sandy Island seems a world away. Its twelve thousand acres are bounded by the Waccamaw River on the east and the Peedee River on the west. No bridges span these waters. Islanders travel to work and children go to school by boat. Once the domain of wealthy rice planters, today the island is inhabited only by wildlife and a handful of African Americans—descendants of the slaves who once worked the adjoining rice fields. In 1990 an attempt was made to bring a highway here, which would have meant the end of Sandy Island's unique natural and cultural features and the beginning of the sprawl that has crept over much of this coastal area. That effort failed, and, at least for outsiders, everything stayed the same.

"Everyone thinks we are the same," an islander says. "Nothing is the same. Our parents worked from season to season. We work from sun up to sun down. Our parents rarely left the island. We seldom are on the island. But our ties to the island are as strong as our parents were. We do not want the island to change, although our lives have changed in so many ways. The island will always be our home."

Daybreak gradually lights the sky along the savanna to reveal an unspoiled landscape. Only moments before, the moon had cast shadows on the mile-long canal that led from the island. With a throb of its outboard motor, a boat appears through the fog. The craft seems to hover as it passes over the waster. A middle-age man wearing steel-toed shoes and a winter parka and carrying a metal lunch box ropes his boat to the dock. A moment later he drives away in the automobile he left parked here. At day's end, he will reverse the trip.

Until fairly recently, families on the island were self-sufficient. All had their vegetable gardens and farm animals: goats, cows, oxen, hogs and chickens. In the woods they trapped small game and hunted deer, wild turkeys, ducks, ricebirds and cooters. The surrounding river supplied shad and freshwater fish. Some still fish for shad. The church has always been the center of the community and remains so. It brings the people together. Sandy Islanders who now live on the mainland return for church services.

Sandy Island is not the same as it was. The Sandy Island of 1940 is hardly recognizable today. Electricity and telephone lines link modern houses to each other. Satellite dishes and television antennas link them all to the modern world. Yet the feeling of the old ways has not been completely lost for a handful of elders who remember the old days and the old ways.

Coming to Sandy Island. *Sandy Island, 1997*

A community leader.
*Sandy Island, 1997*

Visits from the mainland. "Welcome to Sandy Island" reads the sign.
*Sandy Island, 1997*

69

"Mother" of the island—or "Grandmother."
*Sandy Island, 1997*

Church sister.
*Sandy Island, 1997*

Mrs. Elliott and her garden. *Sandy Island, 1997*

## Mrs. Elliott's Yard

In Mrs. Elliott's broom swept yard,
She has raised her children,
Grand children,
Now her great grand daughter.
Her front yard is lined with shrubs and flowers.
*Her* Back yard,
*A* Vegetable garden,
Orderly rows,
With snap peas, collards, and peanut sprouts.

At the water's edge. *Sandy Island, 1997*

Old school building, now a community center. *Sandy Island, 1997*

Praise God for this island.
*Sandy Island, 1997*

Family reunion.
*Sandy Island, 1997*

In the churchyard.
*Sandy Island, 1997*

Pepsi machine in the middle of nowhere.
*Sandy Island, 1997*

Leaving the island. *Sandy Island, 1997*

## A Mirage of the African Savanna

Sons of Kings,
Tall, lean,
Skin the color of the dark soil of Africa.

Their great-grand fathers were bound,
And shipped from Africa.
Still on the river edge,
Their images reflect,
As their great-grand father's image
Reflected on the river edge.

Netting shad.
*Sandy Island, 1997*

Rowing upstream.
*Sandy Island, 1997*

Casting the shad net.
*Sandy Island, 1997*

Shad caught.
*Sandy Island, 1997*

Getting a handle on the shad.
*Sandy Island, 1997*

Onto the boat.
*Sandy Island, 1997*

A gar fish is thrown back. *Sandy Island, 1997*

# The Santee Delta

*These Santee Delta photographs were taken over several years, and are loosely concerned with the resident population. Rice production has long since passed and only a limited "service" economy has come to replace it, so those seeking employment have to commute. Many do. But most of the people pictured here are retired—that is if you can retire from being a grandparent or a churchgoer or simply a community member. Below are Vennie's thoughts.*

*W.B.*

The Santee River enters the ocean fifty miles north of Charleston, and when it does, a large fan-shaped delta is formed. This Santee Delta had been my family's home for generations. Slavery brought my ancestors here as early as 1700. They were brought to work in the rice fields.

A score of plantations were built along the river's banks. It was a wild world of savannas, swamps and maritime forest, inhabited by Indians. The slaves cleared all of this and built fields that could be flooded and drained by the flow or ebb of the tide. This massive land transformation took thousands of slaves. It was their engineering ability that created dikes six feet high and twelve thick and they built the massive wooden trunks that let the water come and go.

These fields are now silent. Rice is no longer grown. The pluff mud clings to the visitor. The cat briar clings. The immense canebrakes bat against the body. The place is still and silent. This is a haunted region. There is no earthly loneliness like that created by my ancestors centuries ago.

Several times I've attended the Episcopal church service in the Village. This is a white congregation and the impression I have is one of haunting. The gentle people. The quietness. Not ghostly, but still haunting. The church goes back to the era of our forefathers, back to the Declaration of Independence, which one member of that church signed. Their ghosts are still there—the one who signed and the other statesmen who also went there. I still have that feeling. The ancestors. I don't mean that negatively. It's just that there's a stillness—in the worship, in the service. I won't say dead. I'm sticking with haunted. There is no spirit in dead.

The black services I attended with my aunt as a child in Charleston were a bit like this. But not here at home. Mama used to tease us with two versions of an old gospel. In my aunt's Charleston church it was "Swing low sweet chariot," and Mama sang it very slow. The McClellanville way, the country way, she sang fast and with rhythm: "Swing low, how sweet the chariot, Oh, how sweet it is to carry me home." The black services around home are definitely not still. No conductors. Spontaneous with voices and testimony all blended. No stillness there.

Curious children. Hand in hand they walk. *King's Highway, 2005*

This church of the Santee planters was built
in 1767.
*King's Highway, 2005*

Church interior. Fantastic light.
*King's Highway, 2005*

Some people say the church is haunted but I don't believe it. *King's Highway, 2005*

Rice barn and mill. A waterwheel provided the power. *Santee Delta, 2000*

## When the Hands Leave the Land

When the hands leave the land,
No more
Human endurance, human strength.

No longer do we work with the tide,
The moon, the seasons.

No longer do we shape the land
With our bare hands,
Molding the earth.
No longer do we hold love to the land.
No longer are we in direct connection
To Mother Nature.
She misses our loving touch.

*Opposite page*: Rice field. *Santee Delta, 2000*

Rice barn and mill interior. *Santee Delta, 2000*

Rice mill gears.
*Santee Delta, 2000*

Rice mill pulley wheels.
*Santee Delta, 2000*

A different kind of interior. The main house of the
Santee Gun Club. Am I really a trophy?
*Santee Delta, 2000*

A second interior. "My father work at the Santee Gun Club.
The big shots came from New York and different places to shoot ducks."
*Santee Delta, 2000*

Fishing at the rice field trunk. *Santee Delta, 2000*

At the strawberry field. *Santee Delta, 2000*

Small boats shrimp at the Santee Delta. *Santee Delta, 2000*

A trunk builder from generations of trunk builders. *Santee Delta, 2000*

"When we were growing up, nothing but woods…"
*Germantown, 2000*

"…Cornfields. Plant a little rice. You couldn't sell it, just something to eat."
*Germantown, 2000*

Sweet shop. "We were sent to the store to buy lunch meat. One pound. Almost ate the whole thing going home."
*Germantown, 2000*

"Hugo came and turned the house around.
My husband slept like a baby."
*Germantown, 2000*

"My granddaddy was a woodman for old man Rutledge." *Germantown, 2000*

"We held onto the land for generations. It will be passed down to our precious grandchildren." *Germantown, 2000*

The senior citizens at the Santee Center.
They raised their children. They even raised their grandchildren.
Now they meet just to enjoy each other.
*South Santee, 2000*

Loving.
*South Santee, 2000*

Tender. *South Santee, 2000*

Sweet.
*South Santee, 2000*

Gentle.
*South Santee, 2000*

After church. *Germantown, 2000*

The church is the hub of the community.
*Germantown, 2000*

"It gives us spiritual strength and more."
*Germantown, 2000*

Mother… *Germantown, 2000*

…and daughter. *Germantown, 2000*

# Hampton Plantation

*A small saltbox structure built by the Horry family as early as 1735 is at the core of this traditional plantation mansion. The great columns, ball room and second story were in place when President Washington came calling in 1793, and the Rutledge family inherited the house and adjoining rice fields soon after. In 1936 the state's poet laureate, Archibald Rutledge, did a romantic restoration of his homeplace and wrote with great love and enthusiasm about the world around Hampton. Forty years later the plantation became a state park and both the flower-laden grounds and newly restored house are open to the public.*

*W.B.*

My grandmother, Lavenia Rutledge Deas, was born on Hampton Plantation. Hampton was the home of the state poet laureate Archibald Rutledge. He was a contemporary of my grandmother and through his prose and poems I have tried to understand the life of blacks here.

Rutledge died in his late nineties and the plantation is now a sate park. The Germantown community just to the north was settled by slaves freed from Hampton and other close-by plantations. The South Santee Community to the south was settled by slaves freed in that region. The photographs I took there were at the senior citizens' center.

My first introduction to the Germantown community was at the Howard AME church and many of those photographs were taken in the churchyard.

A dirt road leading off to other old homesteads. *Hampton Plantation, 2000*

Hampton Plantation. *Hampton Plantation, 2000*

Hampton House stood for over two hundred years. General George Washington stopped here for breakfast in 1793.
*Hampton Plantation, 2000*

"Our community was matriarchal. The men worked hard. The women cared for us." *Hampton Plantation, 2000*

*Camellia japonica.* "So delicate are its petals."
*Hampton Plantation, 2000*

"Fly away." Hampton Plantation's black cemetery.
*Hampton Plantation, 2005*

Francis Marion fought the British here. These are modern-day reenactors. *Hampton Plantation, 2000*

Children reenactors. *Hampton Plantation, 2000*

A glittering reflection. *Santee Delta, 2000*

# Dawson Lumber

The oldest Germantown men said that after the rice planting collapsed they started logging and making turpentine. The trees around them suddenly were a source of income. But then in the 1930s, the U.S. Forest Service bought the land and bigger companies took over. Often the men had to go out of the community to find work.

The pulp mill in Georgetown did start up and is going strong. Still, I was surprised that Dawson Lumber Company was milling logs. Everything is changing. I worked in the Choppee schools above Georgetown. That's the edge of tobacco land, and cotton is growing in the middle of the state, but the old ways of making a living are going fast.

Dawson Lumber. Lumber and tobacco used to be the crops but now it's mostly lumbering. Finished lumber going on its way.
*Georgetown, 2001*

Generations of timber men. *Georgetown, 2001*

Spanish immigrants.
*Georgetown, 2001*

Gloves for handling the lumber and blocking the sun.
*Georgetown, 2001*

Tuning up. *Georgetown, 2001*

Loading the truck. *Georgetown, 2001*

Loading the bins. *Georgetown, 2001*

I couldn't resist this pattern. *Georgetown, 2001*

# Book Three

# People at Home

# Home

Home is a place where black and white are separate and yet connected. There's a closeness. The outside world doesn't matter that much in a community that is this strong.

A Saturday ball game. People come from up and down the streets. There's a little concession store. They simply enjoy themselves. They have good times. This is such an encapsulated environment, it's not just a baseball game. It's a way for the young people to get together. A way for everybody in the community to get together. Another team will come from Santee or Germantown, seven or eight miles up the road.

The Christmas parade probably evolved out of the Lincoln High School Homecoming parade. That high school is so important to the community, and homecoming is one of the biggest events of the year. No matter how long they've been away, some never leave home in their hearts. I've had people tell me they don't even change their car license tags. They stay in New York or Washington their whole adult lives, but still have South Carolina tags. They want to stay attached. Homecoming or Christmas, they want to belong.

One of my earliest memories is of not being home, of my mama not being there. I remember standing in the middle of my Aunt Clara's kitchen. The floor was covered with printed linoleum. A vivid image—me and my brown suitcase and the linoleum. Suddenly my mama was nowhere in sight. I don't remember if I cried. There I stood with the little brown suitcase on the floor. Mama had decided that I would be better off growing up in Charleston instead of McClellanville. I remember Mama taking me into the fields with her. She had to get me out in the world. My hands were too small to pick beans. I think that really is the reason. She didn't think I was tough enough for the country. In the years since, I've surprised her.

Oh, I do remember home. I remember my grandmother. I remember the fields around the houses. I remember a few things, but not like I remember the suitcase. When I was going off to college Mama said I could have whatever I wanted. I got six new blue suitcases. That was my revenge for the brown suitcase. All that Samsonite luggage was my revenge.

A community ballgame on Big Road.
*McClellanville, 1997*

We are going to win this game.
*McClellanville, 1997*

Score keepers. *McClellanville, 1997*

We grew up caring for each other. *McClellanville, 1997*

Christmas parade down Society Road with classic cars.
*McClellanville, 2001*

Beauty queens.
*McClellanville, 2001*

The Sunbeam Choir.
*McClellanville, 2001*

Joy to the World.
*McClellanville, 2001*

## Baby Girl

Birthing,
A baby girl.

Joy,
Poverty.

Her beautiful baby girl,
Hands so tiny,
Not suitable for hard labor.

Her skin so delicate,
Not to bake in the hot sun.

Her body so petit,
Not to carry heavy sacks of cotton.

Kidnap her at night,
Leave her on a gentle lady's doorstep.

## Disinheritance

The sky with millions of stars,
Lit only by the waxing moon.

The nights full with crickets…
Night sounds and spirits.

The light bugs flicking light,
In the darken yard.

The calm breeze airs the gardenia bush,
Sending the fragrance
Through the screened-in porch.

## Bonded

We are bonded by an invisible bondage.
It is taking generations to free us.
Uncertain if we will ever be
Completely free
Of each other.

Classic car driver.
*McClellanville, 2001*

Community activist.
*McClellanville, 2005*

"What beautiful children."
*McClellanville, 2005*

"My daddy built most of the houses in our community."
The Masons, the Braves and a number-one granddad.
*McClellanville, 2005*

She holds onto the land for her children. *McClellanville, 2005*

Mrs. Agnes Brown lived to the age of 106. *McClellanville, 2000*

### Fences: Society Road

Ditch bounded yards,
Chicken wire laced with Four-o-clocks.
Abandoned homesteads,
Old oaks,
And magnolia bushes.

### Paisley Images

A soft ripple,
Of the breeze,
Flows in the stillness,
Of my place.
Paisley Images.

### Fences: Pinckney Street

White picket fences,
Mowed Green Lawns.
c. 1785
Deer head Oak,
And azalea bushes.

### Pinckney Street

Ancient oaks,
Jasmine,
Crepe myrtle,
Camellias,
Along hot concrete sidewalks.

Pinckney Street. Entering that screen door drops you back in time. *McClellanville, 2005*

*Below*: Fourth of July. Founding families and newcomers continue the tradition of celebration. *McClellanville, 2005*

*Above*: Deer head oaks and her tire. *McClellanville, 2005*

Parish priest
*McClellanville, 2005*

Retired warden.
*McClellanville, 2005*

# Africa

I went to Africa with an anthropologist, Andy Gordon. Andy's son Daniel went too and as soon as we arrived he got worms. Nocturnal. Every night they came out of his skin. And each night I had wet wipes to deal with these larvae. Andy was studying cattlemen. He spoke two African languages and French. I couldn't understand anyone, so I went around with my camera. (I also did audiotapes for him without understanding what was being said. A working vacation.)

Because they were Muslims, the women were separate from the men and I usually followed the women. I dressed like them. I had my head covered. Slews of people—children attached to their mothers. They don't run everywhere. I'd get in their midst with the camera. They'd be doing chores. I couldn't understand them. One was photographed breast-feeding and got angry. You can see in the photograph the other girls were laughing at her.

What struck me most, I suppose, was that division of men and women. And also the attitude toward death. We were doing interviews, and if on that day someone in the home had died of cholera, they'd say come back the next afternoon. We have a burial today. Death was such an everyday occurrence.

And there's no waste. There's no garbage, no garbage cans. Astonishing. Everything is used.

Our host, Abu Bakr, surprised me. He and his family lived in the old French Quarter. Abu Bakr served us dinner in a large European-style house and we slept there. But one morning I wanted to help straighten up our quarters and was looking for a bag. I went around the back of the house, and discovered that his family lived in a hut. They preferred that. In the back was a whole new world. France had granted the country independence and then pulled the plug on that civilization. No electricity. The water was cut off so they caught rainwater.

And I was struck by the distinct difference between day and night. Between dark and light. When the sun went down you went to bed. Coming back into America I saw all this neon glowing. Over there night was night. When day comes everybody gets up.

Most importantly, while there I realized that these were people who had life as wealth. They had no external wealth, so they cherished family; I could say they cherished poverty. I know that doesn't make sense, but you have to see that here we have all this waste, all this wealth of material goods and that's what we cherish. There, they cherish what they have. The basics—family, food on the table, clothing. When I went into an adobe hut all I saw was a bed. That made sense. All they did was sleep in there. It's what my mama says: it's not what you want, it's what you need. If you grow up poor you don't know you're poor. It's only when you find out others have more than you that you start to worry. In Africa I didn't see unhappy people. I didn't see people wanting things. Africans cherish life. I did come back a different person.

*Guinea, Africa, 1994*

Guinea, the town of Tyajje. Mother and child inside their tribal compound. *Guinea, Africa, 1994*

Guinea, town of Jonjore. A furniture maker. *Guinea, Africa, 1994*

The town of Tyajje. Outside the compound. *Guinea, Africa, 1994*

Tyajje. We picked bananas and oranges right off the trees, but he's eating an apple. *Guinea, Africa, 1994*

Guinea, town of Pita, in the abandoned French quarter. *Guinea, Africa, 1994*

*Guinea, Africa, 1994*

Women gathering.
*Guinea, Africa, 1994*

146

Irrigation ditch.
*Guinea, Africa, 1994*

A grazing cow inside a karl?
*Guinea, Africa, 1994*

Our host Abu Bakr did speak English. He was the chief. He said he wanted to marry me. I said you're crazy. He had two wives. His father was killed in the revolution and one of his brothers, too, so he inherited that brother's wife. One wife was in the city and the second, the brother's, in the country. She was the one I spent time with, the one who looked after me.

*Guinea, Africa, 1994*

# Pawleys Island

*Four miles long and a half-mile wide, Pawleys Island became a haven for summer vacationers not long after the American Revolution, and today enjoys an almost mythical reputation as a genteelly shabby retreat. Houses can be rented and there are several inns, and for day visitors parking especially at the south end. Pawleys is about sixty miles north of Charleston and about forty miles south of Atlantic Beach, where Vennie went as a child.*

*W.B.*

Summers were predictable—hot, humid, suffocating. Back then, black people were not allowed on the white beaches unless they were maids or yard keepers. Along Ocean Drive, sandwiched between North Myrtle Beach and Myrtle Beach (the "white people beaches"), was Atlantic Beach, the "Negro beach."

When we went there I was told not to go beyond the pier and "those log barriers." As a little girl I can remember disobeying and climbing up those tar-covered logs. They stood far above my head, side by side, lined up like a wall extending out into the ocean. Once at the top I peered over to see a sea of white people. Children were running and playing. Some were building sandcastles. Big beach umbrellas were pitched into the ground, sheltering old white women in huge sun hats. The younger ones were lying on large towels, bare bodies exposed to the sweltering sun. The intense rays made the glittering white sand almost blinding.

Clawing down those hot black logs, I ran back to my family. My mama was preparing lunch. Red rice, white potato salad, green beans. My mama made a picnic table out of the trunk of our large four-door Chevrolet. Reaching for a fried drumstick, I caught my mama's attention; "Child where in the world did you get that tar all over you! Go and wash yourself. Don't go too far and drown!"

I love the beach. Blacks are now allowed on "white people beaches." As an adult I could sit on my beach towel beside the dunes with an oversize straw hat shading me from the sun. I could watch my two sons taking to the ocean like two porpoises.

I dare not get any closer to the breaking surf. Although I lived on the coast all of my life, I was never taught to swim. I was not allowed to wade any deeper than the surf saturating the bottom of my bathing suit. To keep me safe, my mother sat me on the edge of the surf with just my little toes getting a sandy wash.

I took these photographs in 1997 when I was staying on Pawleys Island with friends.

Pier with breaking surf. *Pawleys Island, 1997*

Beach houses. And bird houses. High noon. *Pawleys Island, 1997*

Starfish. *Pawleys Island, 1997*

Friends on the beach. *Pawleys Island, 1997*

The ghost of Alice Flagg searches always
for her ring. But that's not Alice.
*Pawleys Island, 1997*

Fishing on the beach.
*Pawleys Island, 1997*

Children playing beside the fishing pier.
*Pawleys Island, 1997*

Adult relaxing beside the fishing pier.
*Pawleys Island, 1997*

Groin at Pawleys. *Pawleys Island, 1997*

Daybreak in the Lowcountry. *Pawleys Island, 1997*

I sipped tea with "Sister" Peterkin and watched the sun go down. *Pawleys Island, 1997*

# Mama

My mother was born near McClellanville but raised in Charleston. Her mother died when she was a baby. My grandfather was a longshoreman and he remarried. My mama went off to the city but kept her country mannerisms. She came back and married my father. They had nine children. I was the first daughter in the family. Three boys and then me. Mama sent me to Charleston to be raised by my aunt. My dad died of leukemia when I was in college. With help from my brother Bub, Mama kept me enrolled and I went on to have a family and career away from her and home.

Seven years ago the oil stove in Mama's bedroom exploded. She had burns over 60 percent of her body. She had a 20 percent chance of living. But she walked to the ambulance. She refused the gurney. Wouldn't get on the stretcher. She had an incredible will to live. She still has. She actually asked the doctor to operate, which they definitely won't do with that much of a burn. She asked to be saved and she was. That sleeve showing in the photograph is covering her burns. She keeps salve on her arms, keeps them moist. While she was in the hospital I stayed at her side as much as possible. I slept in the waiting room and then in a nearby apartment for another month.

Mama wasn't just a mama to me. When she got burned, the whole community was in a panic. She was a mother of the community So many depended on her. She is Sister Eugenia. She is the nurse, the Da.

Mama worked in the Lincoln High School cafeteria her whole life and then she retired and started a taxi service. She would take people around who had no other way to travel. She would even conduct tours. And her whole life she took care of children. She took care of her own and others. White and black children. That's what the poem "Nipple Confusion" is about. She saw one woman upset in the store and said, bring that child to me. I'll raise him. She did. He was a white child. Her Lukey.

I should add that she has a wicked sense of humor. When somebody who wouldn't work complained about having nothing, she said, "Lay on the ground and let the sky cover you." She hasn't got much patience with that sort of behavior. And when a *National Geographic* photographer came to the house and asked about that triangle shown in the photograph, Mama just said, "Egypt." A photograph of that triangle on the chimney showed up in the magazine as an example of Gullah magic. But my New Age brother from Oregon is the one who painted it on there. He's into crystals and that sort of thing.

I am going to let the poems and photographs say the rest for me. Mama spent her whole life connecting to people. At eighty-one she is still doing that. I want to do the same. Maybe not in the same way, but still connecting. I guess I want to be a person my Mama can be proud of, and I believe she is.

*McClellanville, 2005*

### Yard Cats

Underfoot,
Peeping out of flowerbeds.
Newly born, not yet weaned.

Tom Cat,
Chasing,
Butterflies,
Lizards and snakes.

Ancient breeds licking their calico fur.
We come.
We go.

The yard cats remain,
Watching over the old homestead.
Like watchdogs.

Mama and the blooming hydrangea. If the hydrangea doesn't bloom, someone in the family dies that year. *McClellanville, 2005*

*McClellanville, 2005*

## Shamrock Clovers

Shamrock clover strung together,
How long can I go.

Looking for four leaves,
Pressing it into a book,
If I can find one.

Long enough so I can jump it,
My shamrock clover,
So moist, Irish green.

Next day,
I return to my Shamrock Clovers.
Down on the ground,
So dry, and scribbled.

I have to start all over,
Stringing my Shamrock Clovers.

## Heirlooms

It is not desiring the hardships,
It is learning how to survive.
It is collecting,
The pieces of her life.

Her old dresses,
Her old photographs,
They tiny glass menagerie.

Just anything,
To cling to her being,
Even long after,
She is gone.

## The Raked Yard

Raked yard,
Receives visitors,
Coming and going,

Children,
Playing marbles.

Hop Scots,
Throwing pebbles,
Skipping lines.

Insurance Man's Footprint,
His sole from J.C. Penny's.

Our tiny footprints
In the Sand.

Late afternoon,
Mama comes,
Raking the yard.

It changes,
All the patterns,
To Cist-Cross Lines.

## Rain on the Tin Roof

Every drop so distinct.
Drop, Drop, Drop.

Every drop keeping in time.
Drop, Drop, Drop.

Every drop intensifying.
Drop, Drop, Drop.

Every drop beat like my heart.
Drop, Drop, Drop.

Every drop so calming.
Drop, Drop, Drop.

Every drop stills me to sleep.
Drop, Drop…

## The Village

An environment of stillness.
A force field of time and space.

## Nipple Confusion

My mama fed me.
My five brothers.
My three sisters.
She also breast fed,
The ones she cared for.
We all suckled at her breast.
Black and White.

## Growing House

Shotgun it's called.
A straight hallway.
You shot a gun at the front door.
It hits any walls.
Straight out the back door.
Hitting the gray squirrel in the pecan tree,
Out in the backyard.

Looking from the front yard,
Can't see the hidden floor,
Behind the gable window.

It has a secret door.
It is like a dollhouse,
With childhood adventures.

It changes with time.
As the family grows,
Rooms are added.

Cutting a hole in the outside wall,
To add a room.

As the children leave,
The grandchildren come.
Warmed by old quilts.

They leave.

The old rooms full.
Old clothes.
Old toys.
Old memories.

*McClellanville, 2005*

*McClellanville, 2005*

### Prey

In my mama's yard and her flowers.
Her trees, lizards, her birds…
Blue jays and robins.

Her cats,
The Yellow Tail cat sits quiet,
In the swing yard chair,
…Pretending to sleep.

The blue jay perched,
In the moss covered oak tree,
Hanging over the painted concrete birdbath.

Late evening my mama returns,
The cat is gone,

Blue jay feathers,
Scattered below,
The concrete birdbath.

*McClellanville, 2005*

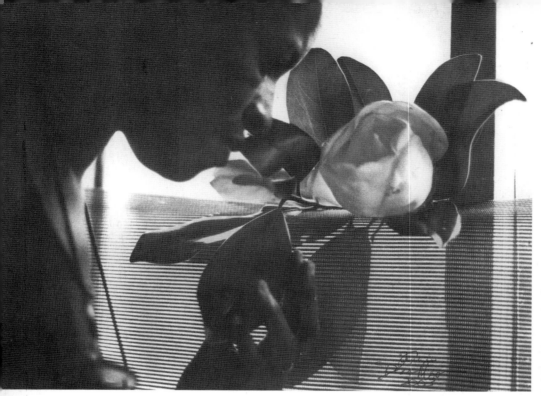

# About the Author

Vennie Deas Moore was born in McClellanville, South Carolina, forty miles north of Charleston. She was educated at the South Carolina Medical University and George Washington University. She currently lives in Columbia, South Carolina. This is her second book.